WHAT IS A PORTRAIT?

A portrait is an image of a particular person, who has usually posed especially for an artist. In this book we'll explore the different ways in which artists can portray people. You will find out what inspired the artists and learn about their techniques. There are also questions to help you look at the portraits in detail, and ideas for creating your own.

◉ You'll find answers to the questions and information about the artists on pages 30-31.

Arty tips

✧ Look out for Arty tips boxes that suggest handy techniques and materials to use in your own work.

Picture hunt

✧ Picture hunt boxes suggest other artists and artworks that you might like to look at.

Early records

Before photography was invented, portraits were made as a record. They would show off a person's wealth, beauty or work, or mark an important event such as a marriage, victory or birth. The settings often gave information about the sitters and their time. This lady, a friend of the French king Louis XV, is lavishly dressed and surrounded by luxurious possessions that hint at her wealth and education. The dog is a sign of her loyalty to the king.

Madame de Pompadour, François Boucher, 1756 (201 x 157cm)

A First Look at Art

Portraits

Ruth Thomson

Chrysalis Children's Books

First published in the UK in 2003 by
Chrysalis Children's Books
An imprint of Chrysalis Books Group Plc
The Chrysalis Building, Bramley Road,
London W10 6SP

Paperback edition first published in 2005
Copyright © Chrysalis Books Group Plc 2003
Text copyright © Ruth Thomson 2003

ISBN 1 84138 703 7 (hb)
ISBN 1-84458-242-6 (pb)

British Library Cataloguing in Publication Data
for this book is available from the British Library.

Editorial manager: Joyce Bentley
Editor: Susie Brooks
Designers: Rachel Hamdi, Holly Mann
Picture researchers: ilumi, Aline Morley
Illustrator: Linda Francis
Photographer: Steve Shott
Consultant: Erika Langmuir, formerly head
of education at the National Gallery, London

The author and publishers would like to thank
the following people for their contributions
to this book: Penny Stevenson and pupils at
St Mary's School, Henley-on-Thames; Laycock
Primary School, Islington; Camilla Bliss-Williams;
Elizabeth Emerson; Rachel Petty; Kate Thackera.

Printed in China

Picture acknowledgements
Front cover: Tate, London 2002 © The Andy Warhol
Foundation for the Visual Arts, Inc./ARS, NY and DACS,
London 2003; 4: Collection of Bayerisches Hypo-und
Vereinsbank AG in the Alte Pinakothek Munich; 5: Scala/
Museum of Modern Art New York/© ADAGP, Paris and
DACS, London 2003; 6/7: AKG London/Galleria degli
Uffizi/Rabatti Domingie; 10, 12tl: Van Gogh Museum,
Amsterdam; 11: Van Gogh Museum, Amsterdam; 14/15, 16tl:
© Marquess of Tavistock and the trustees of the Bedford
Estates; 18/19: Tate, London 2002 © The Andy Warhol
Foundation for the Visual Arts, Inc./ARS, NY and DACS,
London 2003; 22: Bridgeman Art Library; 23: Bridgeman
Art Library; 26/27: AKG London/Erich Lessing/Sko
monastery near Uppsala, Collection Baron R von Essen.

Contents

Changing portraits

After the invention of photography, there was less need for painting to record lifelike details. So many artists started making portraits that were more experimental.

In this striking portrait of himself, Chagall painted his face green and his lips and eye white. He included sights that he remembered from the Russian village where he grew up.

The picture is a jumble of memories, so Chagall painted the people and animals in varying sizes with some of the houses and people upside-down.

I and the Village, Marc Chagall, 1911 (192 x 151cm)

Looking at portraits

When you look at portraits, remember that the artists have made careful decisions about how they show their sitters. Some portraits show a full-length view; others focus on just the face. Some people are pictured in their best clothes; others in everyday dress. Look at people's poses and expressions, which may give clues about their personalities. Look for objects that describe a person's situation or interests. Think about why the portrait was made. Some portraits are large, to impress; others are small, to be carried around.

PEOPLE IN PROFILE

A face seen from the side is called a profile. Run a finger around these profiles. Notice how different they are.

The man's nose is a strange shape, because it was broken in a jousting contest. His right eye was damaged too, so he was always painted in left profile.

The people

Federigo was a brave general and ruler of Urbino, a city in Italy. Battista was his wife. He probably had this double portrait painted after Battista died, to remind him of their life together. The portraits were painted on small panels, hinged together like a book. This meant that Federigo could close them up and carry them wherever he went.

Battista Sforza and Federigo da Montefeltro
Piero della Francesca
c1472 (each panel 47 x 33cm)

The faces

Battista's skin is pale and smooth. In her time, pale skin was seen as a sign of beauty. Some people think her face looks more like a death mask.

◉ How has the artist made Federigo's skin look more realistic?

The costumes

The couple are dressed in their best clothes. Federigo's red robes and matching hat make him look very important.

◉ What do Battista's sparkling jewels and her decorated dress and hair suggest?

The background

The scenery shown here is imaginary, but Piero included the walled town where he was born.

◉ Can you see the town?

LOOKING SIDEWAYS

Paint a friend's profile

- Sit a friend sideways so that you can see only one of his or her eyes and the shape of the nose.
- Draw an outline of your friend's head and shoulders. Paint in the details.

Copy a famous profile

- Paint your own version of Battista Sforza's profile. Glue on some sparkly beads for her jewellery.

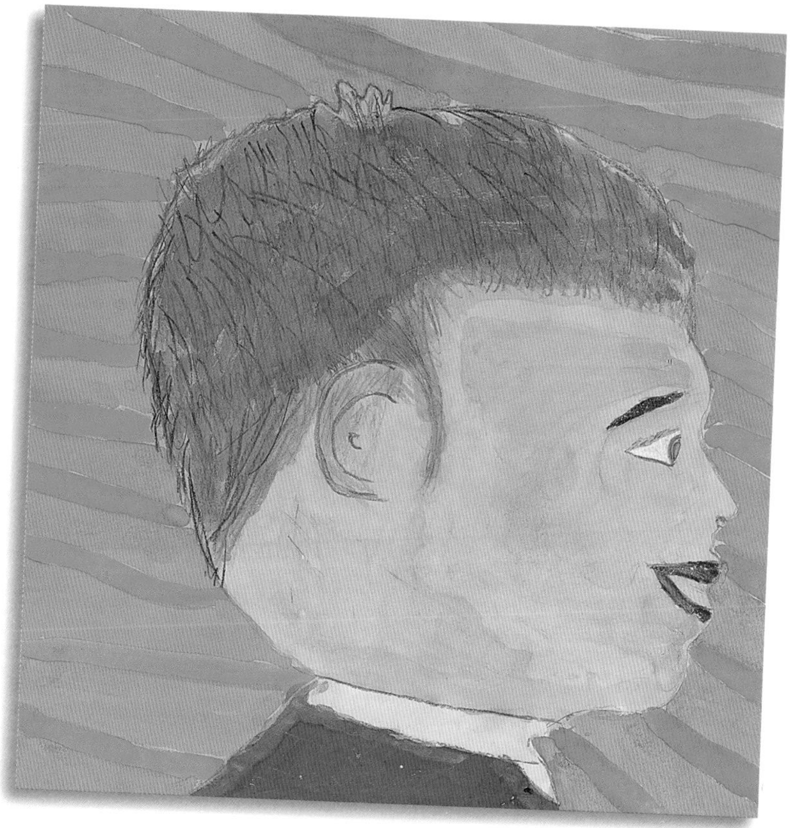

Callum, aged 11

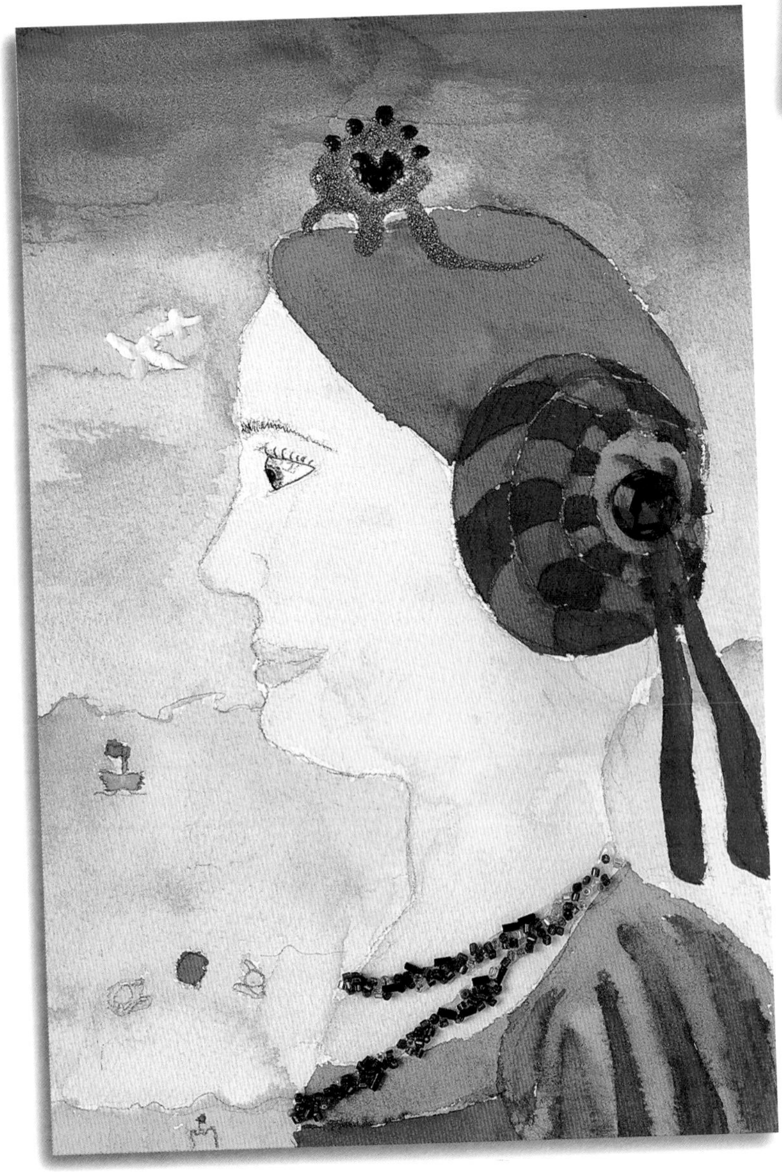

Camilla, aged 12

Arty tips

- Notice how eyes come half-way down the head.
- Remember to include an ear (unless it is hidden by hair).
- The eyebrow is usually level with the top of the ear.
- The tip of the nose is usually in line with the bottom of the ear.

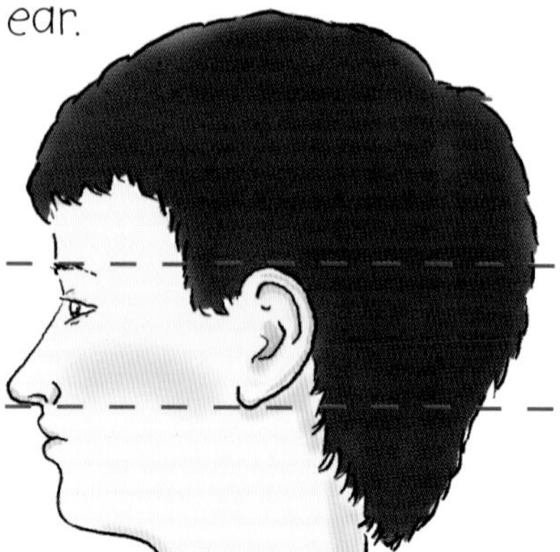

Silhouettes

Before photography was invented, cut-out shadow profiles, called silhouettes, were a cheap way of making portraits. Try creating your own.

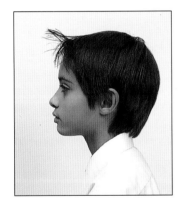

◉ Find a photograph of yourself, or a friend, in profile.

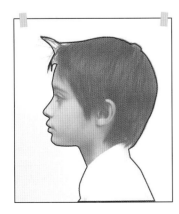

◉ Put tracing paper over it. Trace the outline of the entire head.

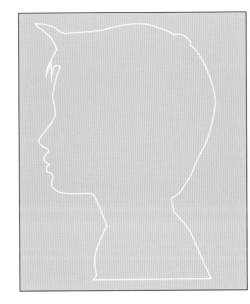

◉ Transfer the outline on to coloured paper.

◉ Cut out the shape.

◉ Use this head as a template for making a gallery of funny faces. Change the shape of the nose, chin, mouth or hairstyle on each head before you cut it out.

angry

happy

scary

WiTCHY

SELF-PORTRAITS

Self-portraits are pictures that artists paint of themselves. These two self-portraits are by the same artist, Vincent van Gogh. He painted them both in Paris, where he went to develop his art and to meet other artists.

Man about town

First, Van Gogh painted himself as a smart city gent, dressed in a suit and hat, out and about at night. The yellow highlights on his face and the swirling, dotted background reflect the bright street lights of Paris. They suggest the movement and noise of a big, bustling city.

◉ What colours did Van Gogh use for the shadowy areas of his face?

◉ How did Van Gogh show the shine on his nose?

◉ How did the artist vary the size of brushstrokes in different parts of his face?

◉ What mood is he in?

Self-Portrait with Grey Felt Hat
Vincent van Gogh
1887 (44 x 37.5cm)

Artist in action

Later, the artist painted himself hard at work in his studio during the day. He has changed into his painter's smock, set a canvas on his easel and squeezed out his paints.

◉ Can you match the colours on Van Gogh's palette with those in his self-portrait?

Self-Portrait in front of an Easel
Vincent van Gogh, 1888 (65 x 50.5cm)

PICTURING YOURSELF

A pastel self-portrait

◉ The direction of Van Gogh's brush-strokes help to give his face shape. Some brushstrokes are laid side by side, some overlap and some criss-cross. Experiment with colour pastels to create your own self-portrait using a similar technique.

Self-Portrait with Grey Felt Hat (detail)
Vincent van Gogh

Aruna, aged 8

Josh, aged 8

Alastair, aged 8

◉ Choose colours that match your eyes and hair. Try, as Van Gogh did, to use a variety of colours for your skin, showing the differing areas of light and shade. Vary the size and direction of your marks, as well.

Moody portraits

◉ What mood are you in today – cheerful, sad angry or worried? Using only black and white paper, cut out a face that shows your mood.

Lily, aged 11

Hannah, aged 11

Leo, aged 11

◉ Paint a self-portrait, showing yourself in the same mood. Use only three or four colours – choose the ones that you think match your feelings the best.

Henry, aged 11

Alexander, aged 11

◉ Include a moody background that emphasises the way you feel. Perhaps use a repeated detail, such as tears, sparks, suns or swooshes.

Picture hunt

✪ Van Gogh was very interested in using colour to express his feelings in paintings. Find other artists who have used colour in this way, such as André Derain, Henri Matisse, Edvard Munch and Howard Hodgkin.

Portraits of kings and queens were often made as a show of power and wealth, or to celebrate an important event. They were meant to inspire the public to be loyal, humble and respectful.

The Armada

This portrait of Queen Elizabeth I celebrates the defeat of the Spanish Armada (warships), which tried to invade England. The scenes in the background show the attack and defeat of the Armada.

On the left, the Spanish fleet is anchored off the English shore. Eight fireships are being sent to drive it away. On the right, the Spanish ships, on their way home, are being smashed against rocks during a fierce storm off the coast of Ireland.

The Armada Portrait of Elizabeth I, George Gower c1588 (42 x 53cm)

Dressed to impress

Elizabeth takes up most of the picture space. She is wearing a rich costume made of the finest satin, velvet, lace and jewels.

⊙ Which parts of Queen Elizabeth's costume make her seem bigger than she really is?

⊙ What shows her immense wealth?

⊙ What two clues identify her as a world ruler?

Flattering looks

When this picture was painted, Elizabeth was 56 years old. She had pock-marked skin, small eyes, black teeth, narrow lips and false hair. She didn't want to be shown like this, so she ordered the artist to make her look agelessly beautiful.

⊙ How did he do this?

⊙ Describe the queen's expression.

PORTRAYING ROYALTY

Face patterns

Elizabeth did not trust most artists to paint the flattering image she wanted. They had to copy officially approved face patterns. These always showed the queen as young and exquisite, even when she was old and wrinkly.

◉ Trace or photocopy this face pattern of the queen. Use it to create your own portrait of Elizabeth I.

The Armada Portrait of Elizabeth I (detail)
George Gower

Lily, aged 11

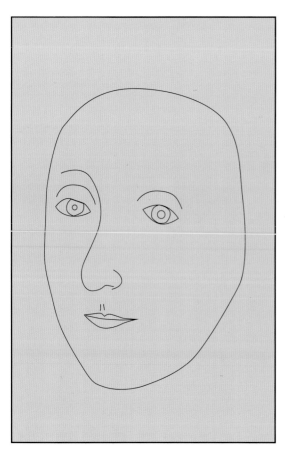

Face pattern of Elizabeth I

Jake, aged 10

Ella, aged 10

◉ Paint a portrait of the queen that she might have approved of, with a white face and red lips.

◉ You may prefer to imagine the clothes and make-up she might wear if she were alive today.

A dazzling dress

Elizabeth had a huge collection of dresses, encrusted with gems or embroidered with gold thread. She wore a different one for each portrait, to create impressive images of her power and greatness.

◉ Make a collage of Elizabeth wearing a glittering costume.

Picture hunt

✫ Find other pictures of Kings and queens and see how many signs of royalty you can spot in them. These might include:

- a crown
- an orb
- medals
- rare jewels
- a coat of arms
- a sceptre
- a sword
- a throne

Gita, aged 9

Alexandra, aged 10

Arty tips

✫ Use patterned fabric for the queen's dress and lace for her ruff (frilled collar).

✫ Add wool or scrap fabric for hair.

✫ Glue on beads, buttons, sequins and other glittery bits as jewels.

✫ Add trimmings of fur or ribbon.

MULTIPLE FACES

Andy Warhol was the first artist to make portraits using machinery to repeat images many times.

Marilyn Monroe

Warhol was fascinated by Marilyn Monroe, a famous 1950s film star who died suddenly at the age of 36. Warhol created this artwork soon after her death.

He took a still photograph from one of her films and repeated it 50 times to create this huge picture.

He used a technique known as silkscreen printing to reproduce the images on to a canvas background.

◉ What is the effect of seeing so many images of the same person at once?

Marilyn Diptych
Andy Warhol
1962 (208 x 145cm)

Garish colours

Warhol chose garish, bold colours to reflect the film posters and adverts of the time.

He used blocks of pure colour to draw attention to Marilyn's dyed blonde hair, her bright eye-shadow and her heavy lipstick.

⊙ What does this use of colour make us think about Marilyn?

Black and white

The black and white images are far less crisp and regular.

⊙ Do you think Warhol smudged and blurred them deliberately?

⊙ Why do you think he made the images on the right become fainter and almost fade away?

REPEATING PORTRAITS

Set of six

◉ Scan a photo or download a digital photo on to a computer.

◉ Using a program that can manipulate images, insert the picture into a new file. Resize it to about 7cm square, so that you can repeat it six times on an A4 page.

◉ Copy and paste the image until you have six. Arrange the six images on your page.

◉ Print the page in black and white, with as much contrast as possible.

◉ Hand-colour each image differently, using clashing colours.

Amber, aged 9

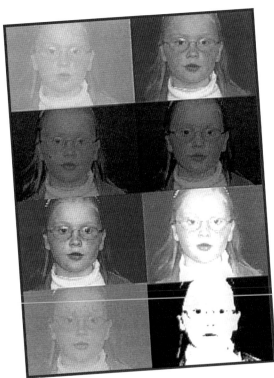

Maddy, aged 9

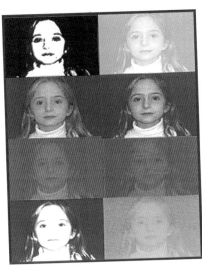

Jennifer, aged 9

◉ Copy and paste the image until you have as many repetitions as you want. Move the images about to create a montage, like these.

◉ Experiment with the buttons on the picture tool bar to change the colours and contrast of each image.

◉ Print out your montage.

Multi-coloured montage

◉ Download a digital picture into a new file on a computer. Insert it into a blank document and resize it.

Me and my mates

⊙ Once you know how to make multiple images of one photo, try combining multiple images of yourself with those of your friends. Experiment with different ways of doing this.

Ryan, aged 11

Conisha, aged 11

Ryan, aged 11

⊙ Reduce or enlarge some of the images.

⊙ Overlap the images.

⊙ Alternate two different images.

⊙ Arrange some of the images at angles.

⊙ Crop some of the images.

⊙ Give the images a border or put them against a coloured background.

Picture hunt

✦ Find other multiple pictures by Andy Warhol, such as:

- Coca-Cola bottles
- Campbell's soup cans
- Marilyn Monroe's lips
- car crashes
- Elvis Presley
- dollar bills

Portraits don't always tell the truth. They can be made to glorify people or things that people have done.

A heroic leader

Napoleon was a famous French general. In 1800, he and his army crossed the Alps and conquered part of Italy. Napoleon trudged along the narrow mountain tracks on a mule, following on several days after his troops. His journey was made in fine weather.

⊙ Which of these facts has the artist changed in his life-size portrait of Napoleon, pictured on the left?
⊙ What effect do these changes have on your idea of Napoleon?

Emperor at work

Napoleon became emperor of France and spent a lot of time making new laws and organising the country's money systems.

In the portrait on the right, there are clues that suggest how hard Napoleon was working on behalf of his people. Napoleon stands in his study, with his ornate desk and gilded, initialled, throne-like chair.

⊙ What time is it on Napoleon's clock? Is it day or night? How can you tell?
⊙ What objects show he has been writing?
⊙ What clues show that Napoleon is still a military leader as well as a ruler?

Napoleon Crossing the Pass of Saint Bernard, Jacques-Louis David 1801 (259 x 221cm)

Napoleon in his Study
Jacques-Louis David
1812 (204 x 125cm)

A HEROIC YOU!

Photo heroes

Soldiers in the early 20th century went to a studio to have their picture taken. The photographer hung up a painted backdrop of a landscape and the soldier posed in front of it.

When a frame was put over the photograph, it hid the edge of the backdrop and the floor. It looked as if the heroic soldier was standing in front of a real landscape.

You can create your own heroic photographs in exactly the same way.

◉ Decide what sort of hero you want to be. Sketch a suitable background for yourself.

◉ Paint a huge version of your sketch as a backdrop. This should

Martha, aged 6

be about the height you are when you stand with your arms stretched above your head. To work out the width, stretch out your arms to either side.

Harry, aged 6

Hugh, aged 6

◉ Dress up in costume, strike a heroic pose in front of your backdrop and ask someone to take your photograph.

Fantastic frames

◉ Once you have a print of your photograph, make a fancy frame for it.

◉ Decide which part of the photo makes you look the most heroic. Draw a rectangle around it and then measure the rectangle.

◉ Cut a card frame with a hole the same size as your rectangle. Paint and decorate the frame.

◉ Fit the frame over the rectangle that you drew on the print. Tape the print to the back of the frame. If the print sticks out at the sides, cut off the edges.

Picture hunt

✬ Find other pictures of heroes. What clues tell you about their achievements? These might include:

- weapons
- fierce animals
- a faraway setting
- important documents
- ships
- an army
- smoke
- a globe

Arty tips

✬ For an embossed (raised) pattern on your frame, mould papier mâché over it.

✬ Alternatively, glue on some straws, dried peas, pasta or lentils in a pattern.

✬ Use silver and gold paint, or foil, to make your frame look very expensive.

Vertumnus, Guiseppe Archimboldo
1590/91 (68 x 56cm)

This head is made up entirely of vegetables, flowers and fruits. It is a portrait of an emperor, Rudolph II. Archimboldo, who painted this, has dressed him up as Vertumnus, the Roman god of vegetation.

Shape and texture

The artist tricks you into seeing the emperor's features by choosing fruits and vegetables that match the face parts in both shape and texture. The furrowed forehead is a wrinkly melon. The shiny nose is a ripe pear. The hairy eyebrows are ears of wheat.

◉ Find what vegetation has been used for the:

- heavy eyelids
- rough beard
- plump cheeks
- spiky moustache
- dangling earring
- muscly neck

Plants and produce

Archimboldo includes produce from all four seasons.

◉ What winter vegetables and autumn fruits can you spot?

◉ What season do the cherries represent?

COLLAGE PORTRAITS

Themed faces

Use Archimboldo's idea to construct some faces of your own. Use objects which have some link with one another, such as nails, screws and washers, or leaves, seeds and berries. Arrange them so that the image can be seen not only as a face, but also as a collection of separate things.

Emma, aged 7

Poppy, aged 8

Picture hunt

✰ Find books with more of Archimboldo's painted faces. See how many different themed objects he used – for example fish, books, weapons or farm tools.

✰ Look out for pictures in magazines (and cookbooks) showing faces made from a collection of real objects that have been photographed rather than painted.

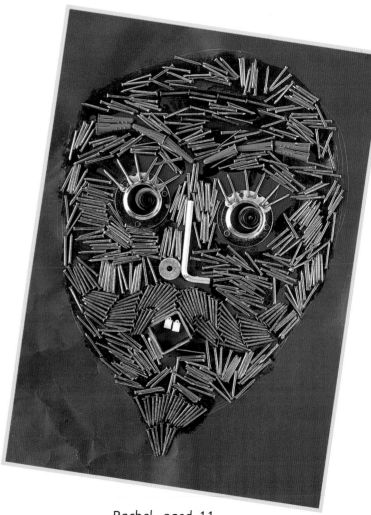

Rachel, aged 11

Cut-out characters

Make a collage face using hair and features cut out of coloured magazine photographs. Take pieces from all sorts of different faces.

Kate, aged 12

Duncan, aged 9

Charlotte, aged 8

Amber, aged 8

Arty tips

✫ To give a face impact, distort the size of some of the features – use a massive mouth or enormous eyebrows.

✫ Cut pieces with a range of skin tones, so you can create areas of light and shade.

✫ Include surprises, such as green hair or a pig's ear!

ARTISTS AND ANSWERS

WHAT IS A PORTRAIT? (pages 4/5)

About FRANÇOIS BOUCHER

Boucher (1703-70) was a French painter who mainly studied in Italy. He painted Madame de Pompadour several times and became chief painter to King Louis XV. He also painted myths and landscapes, designed tapestries and decorated the royal palaces.

About MARC CHAGALL

Chagall (1887-1985) was born in Russia. He studied art in St Petersburg and then in Paris. As well as painting, he designed stage sets and illustrated books. During World War II, he fled to America. He later returned to France and created huge murals and tapestries.

PEOPLE IN PROFILE (pages 6/7)

Answers for page 7

• Wrinkles and warts make Federigo's skin look realistic.
• Battista's outfit shows that she was wealthy and fashionable.
• The walled town is beyond Battista's chin.

About PIERO DELLA FRANCESCA

Piero (c1415-1492) was born in Borgo San Sepolcro, in Italy. The first record of his work is in Florence, where he helped to decorate the walls of a church with religious paintings. For much of his career, Piero painted scenes from the Bible for chapels, palaces, churches and a town hall, in different Italian towns. He worked for some of the most powerful leaders in Italy, including the Pope and two dukes. Piero was a great perfectionist and often spent years on one job. In the last ten years of his life, he gave up painting and wrote about mathematical subjects instead.

SELF-PORTRAITS (pages 10/11)

Answers for page 10

• Van Gogh used dark green and different shades of brown side by side for shadowy areas of his face.
• He painted yellow streaks for the shine on his nose.

• He used short strokes to shape his brow and suggest his bristly beard. He used longer strokes to shape his nose, ear and cheeks. The direction of each stroke helps to define the shape of his face.
• He might be feeling tired, worried, lonely or just thoughtful.

About VINCENT VAN GOGH

Van Gogh (1853-90) was Dutch. He worked as an art dealer, schoolteacher and missionary before becoming a painter. His first works were dark pictures of poor Dutch people. He went to Paris where his brother, Theo, introduced him to French painters such as Paul Gauguin, Georges Seurat and Camille Pissarro. They inspired him to use bright colours and distinct brush-strokes. He then moved to the south of France, where he painted the landscape, his home and his friends. He started having attacks of madness and spent time in an asylum, but carried on painting. He died having sold only one picture in his lifetime.

A MAGNIFICENT QUEEN (pages 14/15)

Answers for page 15

• Elizabeth's neck ruff, puffed sleeves, wide skirt and head-dress make her look bigger than she really is.
• Her jewel-encrusted dress, numerous loops of pearls and other jewels show her immense wealth.
• The crown and globe identify Elizabeth as a world ruler.
• The artist painted Elizabeth with white, unlined skin, large eyes, plump cheeks and full lips to make her look young and beautiful.
• The queen seems very calm, distant and imposing.

About GEORGE GOWER

Gower (1540-96) was an English portrait painter, who worked in London during the 1570s. In 1581, he became Serjeant Painter to Queen Elizabeth I. As well as painting the queen's official portraits, Gower was in charge of decorating all the royal palaces.

MULTIPLE FACES (pages 18/19)

Answers for pages 18 and 19

• The many images of Marilyn may make us see her more as a pattern than a person.

• The garish colours make us think of Marilyn as a glamourous, carefully made-up star and perhaps as rather unreal. The contrast between the colour and black and white images suggests the contrast between life and death.

• Warhol probably smudged, blurred and faded the images deliberately to show that Marilyn had recently died.

About ANDY WARHOL

Warhol (1928-87) was an American who worked in advertising before becoming a painter. His first works were inspired by modern, everyday images in ads and magazines. He stencilled pictures of objects, such as soup cans and Coca-Cola bottles, as well as famous people. From the 1960s, he made films, ran a night club and managed the rock group Velvet Underground. He employed many assistants to help him in his studios, known as 'The Factory'. Fascinated by stardom, Warhol became a celebrity himself and greatly influenced the art of his time.

PORTRAITS OF A HERO (pages 22/23)

Answers for page 23

• Napoleon is shown on a huge, rearing horse, not a mule. He seems to be urging his army forwards, rather than following them. The weather looks stormy, not fine.

• These changes make Napoleon seem forceful, determined and heroic.

• It is 4.13. It must be early morning, since the candles are almost burnt down.

• Napoleon has been writing with a feather quill pen and ink.

• His uniform, medals and sword show that he is still a military leader.

About JACQUES-LOUIS DAVID

David (1748-1825) – a Frenchman – won a prize to study art in Italy. He spent six years drawing antique sculptures and learning about ideas in ancient Rome. Back in France, he painted heroic Roman themes. He became involved in the French Revolution and painted pictures to support it. But when Napoleon came to power in 1799, David supported him instead, and started painting pictures to glorify him. When Napoleon was defeated at the battle of Waterloo in 1815, David fled to Brussels. He died there ten years later.

A MADE-UP FACE (pages 26/27)

Answers for page 27

• Rudolph's eyelids are pea pods; his beard is the spiky case of a sweet chestnut; one cheek is an apple, the other is a peach; his moustache is two hazelnuts in their cases; the earring is a fig; his neck is a mixture of onions, turnips, celery and an aubergine.

• Autumn fruits include black and green grapes, a plum, pears, a pomegranate and hawthorn berries. Winter vegetables include a pumpkin, celery and onions.

• The cherries represent summer.

About GUISEPPE ARCHIMBOLDO

Archimboldo (1527-93) was an Italian painter. He trained in Milan with his father, designing stained-glass windows. From 1562 until 1587, he was the court painter in Prague to three important emperors. As well as painting portraits and decorations for the emperors' rooms, he organised tournaments and wedding feasts, and designed stage sets and costumes. He also collected exotic birds, animals and rare objects for Rudolph II's Art and Wonder Chambers. He is best known for his fantastic heads, made up from fruits, animals, vegetables, tools and other objects.

GLOSSARY

canvas A stiff cloth that artists use to paint on.

collage A picture made by sticking scraps of paper, fabric, or other objects, on to a background.

easel The stand on which an artist rests a canvas.

montage A picture made by placing a selection of images together on a page.

mural A picture that is painted directly on to a wall.

palette The board or other surface on which an artist mixes paints.

pastels Soft crayons that may be either chalky (soft pastels) or oily (oil pastels).

silkscreen printing Printing using a fine silk stencil. Paint is forced through tiny holes in the silk, on to a surface.

smock An over-shirt worn by an artist to protect his or her clothes.

texture How something feels to the touch, for example rough or smooth.

INDEX